The Witch's Complete Guide to Crystals

chartwell
books

Brimming with creative inspiration, how-to
projects, and useful information to enrich your
everyday life, quarto.com is a favorite destination
for those pursuing their interests and passions.

This edition published in 2022 by Chartwell Books,
an imprint of The Quarto Group
142 West 36th Street, 4th Floor
New York, NY 10018 USA

T (212) 779-4972 F (212) 779-6058
www.Quarto.com

10 9 8 7 6 5 4 3 2 1

Chartwell titles are also available at discount for retail,
wholesale, promotional, and bulk purchase. For details,
contact the Special Sales Manager by email at
specialsales@quarto.com or by mail at The Quarto Group,
Attn: Special Sales Manager, 100 Cummings Center
Suite 265D, Beverly, MA 01915, USA.

ISBN: 978-0-7858-4085-5

Library of Congress Control Number: 2022939227

Publisher: Wendy Friedman
Editorial Director: Betina Cochran
Senior Design Manager: Michael Caputo
Editor: Cathy Davis
Designer: Erin Fahringer

Image credits: Shutterstock

Printed in China

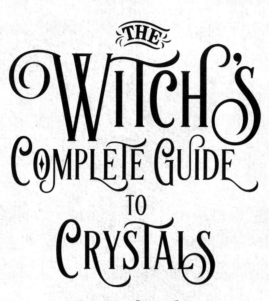

THE WITCH'S COMPLETE GUIDE TO CRYSTALS

A Spiritual Guide to Connecting to Crystal Energy

Sara Hadley

chartwell
books

CONTENTS

INTRODUCTION

HISTORY OF CRYSTALS

Crystal magic dates back centuries to when humans used the elements of nature for healing and other ritualistic purposes. Some crystal origins are tied back to ancient Egypt and India and are still prevalent in Native American culture.

The first written record of the use of minerals dates back to ancient Egypt. Minerals like galena and stilbite were crushed and used for make-up, especially around the eyes. Egyptians also used crystals for their healing properties. Malachite—a copper-based mineral used to clean wounds due to the belief that it has an antimicrobial effect. Other civilizations saw the power of crystals as well. Babylonians used lapis lazuli to ward off evil. Chinese used crystals healing as a form of medicine.

HOW THEY ARE USED IN WITCHCRAFT

Over recent decades, a renewed interest in crystals has emerged, turning what was once an underground world into a highly accessible topic. Healers, Shamans, Energy Workers, Wiccans, and many others continue to use crystals in their practices by connecting us with universal energy through crystals.

There are many tools a witch can use today. One of the oldest is crystals. Crystals are naturally occurring materials with highly ordered atoms and a constant vibration. People throughout time have included crystals in their medicinal practices, religions, and ritual use.

In the magical world of vibrations, crystals can aid you along your spiritual journey through intention setting. Any witch will tell you that is an essential step in witchcraft. As witches, we lean into the energies of the crystals. They can be used to add magic to the mundane—like using crystal-charged water for your coffee. In this book, we will be exploring different ways to use crystals to enhance your everyday rituals and spell work.

1

CONNECTING TO CRYSTALS

CHOOSING YOUR CRYSTALS

Finding the right crystal can seem like a daunting task with thousands of crystals to choose from. Just remember to let your intuition guide you!

Finding a crystal can sometimes be overwhelming, especially if you are just starting. There are thousands of different stones, all with their own properties and benefits. If you are lucky enough to have a local crystal or metaphysical store, we suggest starting there. Staff can help guide you and is knowledgeable. There are also many reputable sellers online, but like anything, make sure you do your research. All sellers should be able to tell you the origin of their material to ensure authenticity and ethical mining practices.

You may want to do some research before you go crystal shopping. If you have a particular aspect of your life you would like work on, look up what crystals you can obtain to support that. For example, if you have been dealing with anxiety lately, research may guide you to select a crystal-like lepidolite or lithium quartz. Both have been touted to ease the anxious mind and provide soothing energy.

Some prefer to skip the internet search and let their intuition guide them. There are a few different tricks you can use to detect the subtle energy of crystals. You can shop by seeing what calls to you. Often you will find yourself drawn back to a particular crystal repeatedly. Pick the crystal up and hold it in a closed hand when this happens. How does it make you feel? Do you notice any physical sensations in your hand, or does it feel like it is giving off heat? Yes? You have found a match!

Instead of using your eyes to see what calls to you, some prefer to base their selections solely on the energy they feel. The crystal's vibration will begin to speak to you the more you become comfortable using it. Over time, as you fine-tune your intuition, selecting your crystals will become second nature by recognizing their healing energies through touch.

You can also let the universe take control ! Use a crystal oracle deck and intuitively select a card for your next crystal. If you don't have an oracle deck, turn to this book's "crystal quick guide" section. Flip through the pages and turn to a random page–that's your crystal!

Once you think you've found the crystal right for you, hold it in your hand and close your eyes. Relax your body and your mind, and ask if this crystal is meant for you; if your body leans forward, it is a yes. If it leans back, try a different selection. The most important thing to remember is that there is no right or wrong way to make your crystal selections.

EXERCISE

Rub your hands together for about a minute, so they are tingly and ready to receive energy. Hover your hands a few inches over the crystals, close your eyes and move them across the table. Turn your attention to any shifts in energy you might feel—do you feel a magnetic-like, or feel any new sensations? Then you have found a match!

CRYSTALS

Several crystals are a must-have for every witch's collection. The following crystals are versatile in spell work, easy to find, and affordable. It's always suggested to shop brick and mortar—however, find a reputable source when purchasing online.

AMETHYST

"THE CLAIRVOYANT"

Amethyst has been shrouded in magical lore throughout history. First discovered in France thousands of years ago, it is still unclear how long it has existed. In ancient times, royalty would drink wine from goblets encrusted with amethyst, the stone of sobriety. They believed it would ward off intoxication and allow them to keep a clear head while their guests indulged.

Amethyst is also regarded as a highly spiritual stone. It can aid the deepening of meditation, opening the third eye, and crown chakras as well as being soothing and providing peace.

Amethyst was once a highly precious stone, symbolizing royalty. The British royalty adorned scepters and crowns with beautiful jewels to symbolize prestige. Catholic bishops and priests wear rings of amethyst to symbolize their abstinence from alcohol and to provide spiritual protection. In the early nineteenth century, amethyst was discovered in Brazil, making it a more accessible gemstone. Amethyst is also regarded as a highly spiritual stone. It can aid in the deepening of meditation, opening the third eye and crown chakras, and being soothing and providing peace. Today we can find amethyst in jewelry, carved into shapes and in raw forms.

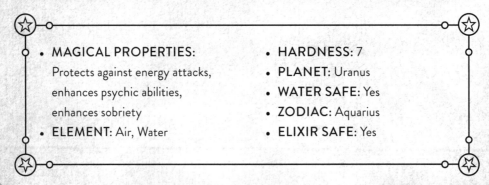

- **MAGICAL PROPERTIES:** Protects against energy attacks, enhances psychic abilities, enhances sobriety
- **ELEMENT:** Air, Water
- **HARDNESS:** 7
- **PLANET:** Uranus
- **WATER SAFE:** Yes
- **ZODIAC:** Aquarius
- **ELIXIR SAFE:** Yes

Clear Quartz

"THE MASTER HEALER"

Clear quartz can be found worldwide and is known as the most renowned of the quartz family. It is a natural form of silicon dioxide that is most found in sedimentary rock but can also be found in other minerals.

Quartz has been a valued crystal by many ancient civilizations as far back as Atlantis. Greek philosophers believed this stone was a form of eternal ice that could not be thawed. It is called Tama or "the perfect jewel" in Japan and symbolizes purity. Romans and Egyptians wore jewelry adorned with clear quartz to signify power. In middle eastern cultures, quartz is held highly as an invaluable crystal used for healing and energy work.

This extremely durable gem with a hardness score of seven is currently used in modern technology. TVs, watches, and even your cell phone contain quartz.

It is known as "the master healer" on a spiritual level due to its versatility and ability to balance all chakras. Clear quartz acts as an amplifier and will bolster other crystals' properties all while absorbing negative vibrations. This makes quartz a quintessential healing tool you will want for your collection!

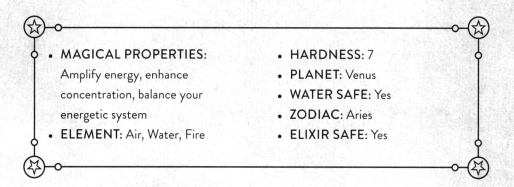

- **MAGICAL PROPERTIES:** Amplify energy, enhance concentration, balance your energetic system
- **ELEMENT:** Air, Water, Fire
- **HARDNESS:** 7
- **PLANET:** Venus
- **WATER SAFE:** Yes
- **ZODIAC:** Aries
- **ELIXIR SAFE:** Yes

TOURMALINE

"THE PROTECTOR"

Tourmaline's discovery dates to the 1500s. It became recognized as a mineral by the 1800s. The name Tourmaline is derived from the Sinhalese term "turmali" due to the confusion of finders mistaking it for other gemstone species.

Its range of color variety makes it truly unique—from red, minty green, blue, and even raspberry pink tones, this striking crystal does not disappoint! Rarely is it colorless. The most commonly found variety is "schorl," which is black tourmaline. Today it is primarily mined for in Brazil and Africa but can be found in Tanzania, Madagascar, Afghanistan, Sri Lanka, and Pakistan.

Tourmaline is a balancer of the yin and yang and is often used in Feng Shui to create an energetic shield around a room to prevent unwelcome energies from entering.

Tourmaline, revered as a highly protective stone, can transmute anything in your life (physically or spiritually), keeping you from your divine purpose.

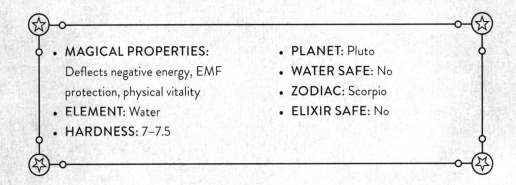

- **MAGICAL PROPERTIES:** Deflects negative energy, EMF protection, physical vitality
- **ELEMENT:** Water
- **HARDNESS:** 7–7.5
- **PLANET:** Pluto
- **WATER SAFE:** No
- **ZODIAC:** Scorpio
- **ELIXIR SAFE:** No

SELENITE

"THE PURIFIER"

Selenite is a crystallized form of gypsum that has been around for thousands of years. Gypsum is a naturally occurring mineral that forms from water evaporating in mineral-rich environments. Selenite was named after the Greek goddess of the moon, Selene. While having roots in Greek Mythology, this crystal was popular in the Mesopotamian culture. They incorporated selenite in ritual practices as well as to ward off evil spirits from the sick. Ancient Egyptians believed that burying this angelic stone in tombs would help the dead pass into the afterlife.

In 1794, the Naica mine was discovered in Chihuahua, Mexico. A chamber within this mine called the Crystal Cave of Giants contains captivating selenite growths up to fifty feet long and four feet in diameter.

A precious stone by crystal enthusiasts and energy workers alike, selenite is optimal for aura cleansing to clear blockages and balance the chakra system. Selenite's pure, yet high vibrational frequency brings peace and harmony while encouraging the natural ebb and flow.

- **MAGICAL PROPERTIES:**
  Purifying, cleansing, harmonizing
- **ELEMENT:** Water
- **HARDNESS:** 2
- **PLANET:** Moon
- **WATER SAFE:** No
- **ZODIAC:** Cancer
- **ELIXIR SAFE:** No

Rose Quartz

"THE LOVE STONE"

Heralded as a talisman of love and relationships, Rose Quartz is a pink variety of mineral quartz. It was found as early as 600–700 BC. Egyptians, Greeks, and Romans used this stone in talismans to symbolize ownership. In Greek Mythology, Rose Quartz is connected to the Greek Goddess Aphrodite. It was believed that during a fight with Ares her blood stained the crystal pink.

To this day, Rose Quartz can be found in intricate carvings throughout China. Gua Shua and crystal combs made out of Rose Quartz have become more mainstream in beauty regimens. Historically, pregnant women believed that keeping rose quartz close by would provide ease through their pregnancy and childbirth. It has also been associated with fertility and conception.

Keeping Rose Quartz close to your heart will facilitate self-love. It is unsurprisingly the best heart chakra and heart-healing stone. It's also excellent for encouraging reconciliation and empathy. Wearing it as jewelry or carrying it in a tumbled form in your pocket will bring a sense of inner peace.

- **MAGICAL PROPERTIES:** Stimulates love of self, heals a broken heart, helps foster forgiveness
- **ELEMENT:** Water
- **HARDNESS:** 7
- **PLANET:** Venus
- **WATER SAFE:** Yes
- **ZODIAC:** Taurus, Libra
- **ELIXIR SAFE:** Yes

CLEANSING

Anytime you get a new crystal, you will want to cleanse and activate it. Just like choosing your crystals, there are several ways to do this. You will find that a common theme in this book is to follow your intuition—there is no right or wrong way!

Smoke Cleansing

ELEMENT: FIRE

 Smoke cleansing is the most common form of cleansing crystals. This method is safe for all of your gems. You can use a few different things to create smoke. Dried herbs and flowers like sage and lavender, incense, or resin all work very well. You will also need a fireproof dish and matches or a lighter.

Set fire to your smoke source and let the flame die down to a smolder; this should produce a steady stream of smoke. Be sure to hold it over the fireproof dish to avoid rogue embers. Start by cleansing yourself; envision a white light radiating out of the top of your head, enveloping your entire body. Move the smoke around your body–head to toe, front and back, allowing it to absorb any negative energies and wash away old stagnant ones. Next, move on to your crystals. One by one, move them into the smoke, allowing it to wash over the entire stone. You can use a mantra like:

May this smoke wash away any energies that do not align with my highest good.

You can keep it that simple or be as creative as possible! Envision the old energy being drawn out of the stone until it shines brightly. Once you have cleansed all your crystals, place the incense, herb bundle, or resin in the fireproof dish, and keep it there until the smolder is out and it is safe to put away.

Water Cleansing

ELEMENT: WATER

 Using running water is another great method of cleansing. This one, however, is not safe for all crystals. It is essential to know whether or not your gem is water safe; you can refer to the crystal quick guide or the recommended online resources in the back of this book.

A general rule is if it ends in "ite" (fluorite, selenite, halite, etc.) or if it has a Mohs hardness of less than six, it should not be submerged in water. This can cause them to crack, break, discolor or dissolve. See Mohs Hardness Scale description below.

Start by cleansing yourself and washing your hands. While you do so, envision any negative energies being drawn out of your body through your hands; watch as they get sucked down the drain, cleansing you thoroughly. Next, move on to your crystals. Take each one placing it under the running water, the same way you cleansed yourself, and imagine all unwanted energies being drawn out of the crystal and being washed away down the drain. Be sure to dry your crystals completely.

Mohs Hardness Scale

MINERAL NAME	SCALE NUMBER	COMMON OBJECT
Diamond	10	
Corundum	9	
Topaz	8	8.5 Masonry Drill Bit
Quartz	7	
Orthoclase	6	6.5: Steel Nail
Apatite	5	
Fluorite	4	
Calcite	3	3.5: Copper Penny
Gypsum	2	2.5: Fingernail
Talc	1	

INCREASING HARDNESS

The Mohs scale is a useful tool in determining the resistance or hardness of your crystals. The range is from 1-10, 1 (softest) and 10 (hardest). This resource can be found online and will come in handy when learning which crystals are water safe depending on their level of hardness.

Burial Cleansing

ELEMENT: EARTH

Using the earth to cleanse my crystals is my favorite method and safe for all gems. First, start with grounding yourself. Take your shoes off and keep your feet flat on the ground. Take a deep breath and exhale. As you exhale, imagine roots shooting down from the bottom of your feet to the earth's center. With every breath you draw in, receive power from the earth's core, and with every exhale, those roots grow deeper and deeper. If you don't have space outside to do this, that is okay. The intention is still the same, so the connection is there. Do this for ten breaths. When you are done, take your crystals and hold them to your heart, ask that the earth cleanse them. You can use the below mantra or go with your own.

Mother Earth, I remit these stones back to you. May you cleanse them of any impurities and restore them of their energies

Bury your crystals in a place you will remember. If access to outdoor space is limited, use a potted plant–just make sure that the stones are completely covered in earth. Keep the crystals buried for at least three days, or you can use the moon's phases as a guide. Bury on the full moon and retrieve on the new moon.

Sound Cleansing

ELEMENT: AIR

Using sound to cleanse your crystals is the easiest method used on all crystals. You will need either a singing bowl, tuning fork, bells, or chimes. Cleanse yourself by sweeping the sound over you, head to toe, front, and back. Imagine the sound penetrating your body and driving out any negative energies, allowing white light to fill you up until it emanates. Move on to your crystals; if you use a singing bowl, you can place the crystals inside as you play it. Envision the sound wrapping around the crystals, absorbing any unwanted energies before the sound fades away.

Sunlight and Moonlight Cleansing

An easy yet powerful way to cleanse crystals is by using the light from our Sun and Moon. You can charge and restore their energies by placing them under a full moon, keeping them on the windowsill for a day to soak in the sun's rays (too much sun exposure can cause color fading), or burying them outside from dusk until dawn. You will want to revisit your crystals periodically for cleansing and charging. Some other means of cleansing are the moon, sun, salt, rainwater, or even other crystals. You can charge them and restore their energies by placing them under a full moon, keeping them on the windowsill for a day to soak in the sun's rays (too much sun exposure can cause color fading), or burying them for twenty-four hours.

Programming

Once you have cleansed your crystals you will want to program or dedicate them. If you haven't done so already, you will want to research your stones.

Every crystal has its own properties to aid in our spiritual, emotional, and physical well-being.

QUARTZ
CLARITY

AMETHYST
RELAXATION

FLUORITE
FOCUS

Once you know what your crystal can do, you want to tailor it to your specific needs. Spend some time meditating with your crystal, and see the benefits you wish to reap in your mind's eye.

For example, if you are working with a tiger's eye, a stone whose properties include keeping one grounded and providing strength and courage, picture yourself in control of a situation where you would typically take a back seat. Tell the universe what you want the crystal to aid in, be specific. Allow the crystals to act as a talisman. It will be a reminder of where you want to be in life and can provide the support to adjust your energy accordingly.

There are several different ways you can program your crystals:

 **VISUALIZATION:** Take your crystal and bring it to your third eye. While focusing on your crystal and intention, repeat the words out loud or in your head "I am programming this crystal with the intent of _____."

 MEDITATION: Find a quiet undisturbed place to sit and and see the benefits you wish to reap in your mind's eye. Do this meditative process for as long as you feel it takes to accomplish your desired programming.

 CRYSTAL GRIDDING: Arranging your crystals in a grid formation on a geometric shape will direct the energy of your intention. You can use Clear Quartz as the generator (center stone) to charge other crystals on your grid. *See more about crystal gridding in chapter 4.

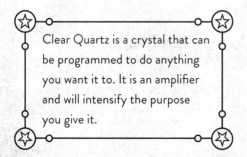
Clear Quartz is a crystal that can be programmed to do anything you want it to. It is an amplifier and will intensify the purpose you give it.

2
CRYSTAL TOOLS

Crystals come in a large selection of shapes and sizes for various metaphysical purposes. This chapter will look at some of the most common and useful tools. While raw crystals and tumbles (see page 41 on tumbled crystals) are great when incorporating the magical properties, they hold onto your everyday life. Certain shapes can amplify your intentions in energy work.

Pendulums

A pendulum is a chain or a string with a weight tied to each end. Crystals, stones, or pendants are commonly attached to silver chains. They are a fantastic tool for tapping into your subconscious. Some believe these tools are the link to connecting us to the answers already known within. There is evidence that ancient healers used pendulums for dousing and divination, and it is believed that these tools may predate history.

Dowsing is a form of divination that provides answers or can assist in finding lost objects. All you need is a pendulum and your intuition to be pointed in the right direction.

Witches today continue to find the pendulum one of the most useful tools in their arsenal. Like any crystal, when selecting your pendulum, choose one based on your intuition. Is there one that you are continuously drawn to? To pair your energy with every new pendulum, you may want to sleep with it under your pillow or on your nightstand.

Before you jump right into asking your questions, you will want to set a baseline. Every person and every pendulum can be different in how the responses are shown. Start by clearing your mind and taking a few deep breaths. Ask your pendulum to show you "yes" and then to show you "no." After asking these questions, the pendulum may swing clockwise, counterclockwise, up and down, or side to side after asking these questions. Do this a few times until you feel confident in recognizing the pendulum's swing for these fundamental questions.

Get your baseline read by starting with questions you know the answers to. "Is my name_____?" While holding it with a steady hand, watch how the pendulum swings. This will confirm the meaning of the pendulum's movements. After doing this a few times, you can start to ask questions you don't know the answers to.

Modern-day witches continue to use pendulums for dowsing, a searching technique. Whether you're looking for your own crystals on a mountainside or your lost keys in your house, you can use crystal pendulums to help locate what you are seeking. Hold your pendulum out and envision what you are looking for. The pendulums will move as you get closer to the object. It's similar to a game of hot or cold played with the universe.

Exercise/Game

Practicing with other witches is a fun way to practice your divination skills with a pendulum. Grab a friend, have them think of a number from one to twenty-five and have them hold that number in their mind. Hold your pendulum out, and one by one, ask if they are thinking of each number. Their answer to you should be "no," even if you've said the correct number. The swing of your pendulum should reveal your partner's number and detect their lie! Take turns guessing, and remember that your skills will continue to improve with practice!

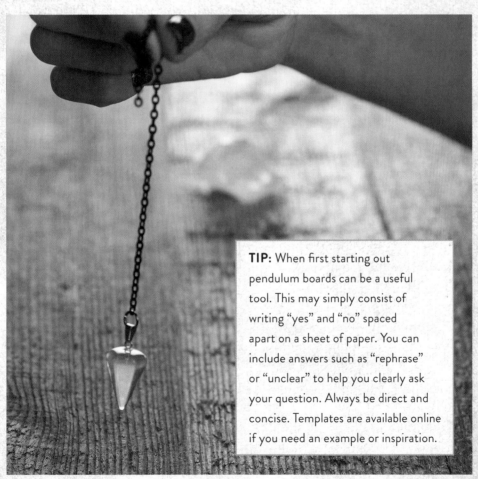

TIP: When first starting out pendulum boards can be a useful tool. This may simply consist of writing "yes" and "no" spaced apart on a sheet of paper. You can include answers such as "rephrase" or "unclear" to help you clearly ask your question. Always be direct and concise. Templates are available online if you need an example or inspiration.

CRYSTAL WAND

Crystal wands are a wonderful tool in energy work. They are used to direct energy flow and can amplify one's intentions. Many energy healers use crystal wands to clear and align the chakras or energy centers of the body. Crystal wands come in just about every mineral out there. Clear Quartz, known as the master healer of crystals, is one you will want in your witch's toolbox. It can be programmed with any intention. When used in crystal grids, spells, or the body itself, it will absorb, amplify, and direct energy.

You can get a little crafty by affixing a crystal to a branch to create your own customized crystal wand. Use glue or crafting wire, and be sure to secure it well. Feel free to decorate your wand with other elements or crystals to your liking.

Exercise

To clear and align your chakras with a crystal wand, start off by setting the intention of balancing your energy. You may want to begin with meditation or taking a few deep cleansing breaths while sitting comfortably or lying down. Starting at the Root Chakra, work your way up to the crown. Use your wand to trace a circle around the chakra you are working with, and envision the wand drawing out blockages and any old stagnant energies until it radiates bright light. Continue this exercise with each chakra.

RED = Root

ORANGE = Sacral

YELLOW = Solar Plexus

GREEN = Heart

BLUE = Throat

INDIGO = Third Eye

WHITE = Crown

CHAKRAS: Chakras (originating from the Sanskrit word for wheel) are energy centers that run in ascending order from the crown of your head to the base of your spine. The seven major chakras are Crown, Third Eye, Throat, Heart, Solar Plexus, Sacral and Root. When all chakras are balanced, energy can move freely harmonizing the body, mind, and spirit. If one or more chakras are blocked or unbalanced, other chakras may overcompensate throwing us out of energetic alignment.

VOGELS

Founded and first cut by Marcel Vogel, a scientist and energy healer, Crystal Vogels is a faceted double terminated wand used to send and receive energy in healing work. The Vogel's double terminations consist of a smaller receptive end, sometimes referred to as the female end of the crystal, and the transmitter, also known as the male end. These wands are designed with a specific cut and shape to increase healing power and transmit Universal Life Force energy.

Although Vogels are traditionally made from Clear Quartz, you can also find them in various crystals such as Smokey Quartz, Amethyst, and Citrine. Dr. Marcel believed that the sacred geometry in Vogels was necessary to assure that energy was attracted, amplified, and appropriately extracted.

Once you hold a Vogel in your hand for the first time, you're sure to feel the energy of this powerful crystal!

Self-healing Exercise

A Vogel can assist in releasing unwanted energy or tension in the body. Before using your Vogel, make sure you have cleansed it by any methods mentioned earlier in this book. (Sage, Smoke, Water, Dirt, Visualization, etc.)

Begin by sitting or lying comfortably. Take three deep, slow inhales and exhale through your nose. Do this several times until you feel calmer and at peace. Start to visualize in your mind the area of your body experiencing discomfort. Holding the Vogel with the larger side (operating tip) up in your hand, begin a scooping motion near the area as if you are getting rid of the pain/discomfort by drawing it from your body. This is known as energetic extraction. Repeat this day and night to help alleviate the stress or tension you feel. Remember to work with intention while using your crystals for the best results.

TUMBLES

Tumbled stones start as raw crystals put through a tumbling process to smooth and polish them. The tumbling process does not take away from the crystal's energetic or vibrational properties. While using raw crystal tumbles vs. polished crystals is a personal preference, tumbled stones are easier to handle and wear on your person, such as in your pocket or bra. Whether it is a small or large tumble, you will receive the same energy, as the size does not matter. Tumbles are easily accessible and tend to be more affordable for a Witch starting out their spiritual journey.

Crystal grids can be set up using tumbled stones. Because of their compact size, you can easily set up a crystal grid in a smaller space or have a portable travel grid for on the go. (We will dive deeper into crystal grids later in the book).

Tumbles are also an excellent choice for energy work such as Reiki. Placing them on or near your client's body will facilitate the energy flow.

Some choose to meditate with tumbles by either holding them in their palm or aligning them alongside or around themselves.

However, if you choose to use your stones, set an intention that coincides with the crystal's metaphysical properties. This will enhance all areas of your spellwork and rituals.

Charging Plates

Now that you have your crystal collection and use them regularly, it's time to get a new tool. To cleanse, charge and amplify the properties of your crystals at once, you are going to want a charging plate.

Selenite slabs or dishes are a fantastic choice! Selenite, a crystallized form of gypsum, unlike any other crystal, doesn't need to be cleansed or charged and will amplify the energy/vibration of the crystals placed on it. The high vibration of Selenite is like pure light. (Be sure to keep your selenite dry as it is a soft mineral and could disintegrate!)

Tip: If you wear crystal jewelry daily, take it off at night and place it on your charging plate to cleanse and clear any negative energy you may have picked up throughout your day.

CRYSTAL SPHERES

The mysterious crystal ball (or sphere) can be spotted in many movies throughout pop culture (*Labyrinth*, *The Wizard of Oz* and *The Little Mermaid* to name a few). This divination tool dates to Celtic Druids, who used it for crystallomancy. It's believed that staring into the stone will open the subconscious mind to receive messages from the past, present, and future. This is also known as scrying.

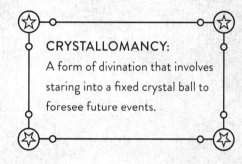

CRYSTALLOMANCY:
A form of divination that involves staring into a fixed crystal ball to foresee future events.

Aside from their smooth and appealing aesthetic, crystal spheres make a wonderful tool in energy healing by sending out energetic light in all directions. Using them in gridwork as the keystone (center crystal) will amplify the manifestation set for your grid. Holding a sphere in your hand during meditation can aid in dropping deeper into a meditative state.

No matter how you use it, set the intention for any crystal sphere and notice the energy shift around you!

"Crystals have been used for centuries to promote serenity and as a tool for meditation. They can be helpful allies in our quest for calm."

— *Amy Leigh Mercree*

3

CRYSTALS AND THE WHEEL OF THE YEAR AND MOON PHASES

"The Moon will guide you through the night with her brightness, but she will always dwell in the darkness in order to be seen."

—Shannon L. Alder

The Wheel of the Year

The wheel of the year is a modern sacred calendar aligned with nature linking the four changing seasons, and is celebrated with eight primary rituals known as sabbats. These sabbats are Yule, Imbolc, Ostara, Beltane, Litha, Lughnasadh, Autumn Equinox, and Samhain. Historically in ancient cultures, spiritual practices were connected to agricultural practices. The Neo-Pagan Wheel of the Year is used to return to old ways of connecting with the land. Modern-day witches continue to celebrate each sabbat by showing gratitude for [the natural and physical worlds] mother earth and all that she provides.

Aligning and planning your rituals to correspond with the sabbats can be a great learning experience in your spell work while using your crystals.

Yule/Winter Solstice

NORTHERN HEMISPHERE: December 19th–23rd
SOUTHERN HEMISPHERE: June 21st
HERBS: Cinnamon, Clove, Pine
CORRESPONDING CRYSTALS: Clear quartz, Citrine, Emerald
COLORS: Gold, Green, Red, Silver, White, Yellow

IMBOLC

NORTHERN HEMISPHERE: February 1st–2nd
SOUTHERN HEMISPHERE: August 1st–2nd
HERBS: Chamomile, Rosemary, Witch Hazel
CORRESPONDING CRYSTALS: Turquoise, Amethyst and Citrine
COLORS: White, Pink, Green, Yellow, Brown, Gold

OSTARA/Spring Equinox

NORTHERN HEMISPHERE: March 19th–23rd
SOUTHERN HEMIPSHERE: September 21st–23rd
HERBS: Honeysuckle, Lemon Balm and Lillies
CORRESPONDING CRYSTALS: Rose quartz, Agate, Jasper
COLORS: Green, Pastel Colors, White, Yellow

BELTANE/MAY DAY

NORTHERN HEMISPHERE: April 30th–May 1st

SOUTHERN HEMISPHERE: October 31st–November 7th

HERBS: Dandelion, Primrose, Rose

CORRESPONDING CRYSTALS: Sunstone, Malachite, Rose Quartz

COLORS: Red, White, Summer Colors

LITHA/SUMMER SOLSTICE

NORTHERN HEMISPHERE: June 19th–23rd

SOUTHERN HEMISPHERE: December 21st–December 22nd

HERBS: Lavender, Sage, Rosemary

CORRESPONDING CRYSTALS: Calcite, Yellow Topaz, Emerald

COLORS: Blue, Gold, Green, Orange, Red, White, Yellow

LUGHNASADH/LAMMAS

---•---

NORTHERN HEMISPHERE: Aug 1st–2nd
SOUTHERN HEMISPHERE: February 1st–February 4th
HERBS: Clover, Basil and Ivy
CORRESPONDING CRYSTALS: Amber, Tiger's Eye, Peridot
COLORS: Bronze, Brown, Gold, Green, Orange, Tan, Yellow

Autumn Equinox

NORTHERN HEMISPHERE: Sep 20th–24th

SOUTHERN HEMISPHERE: March 21st

HERBS: Rosemary, Chamomile, Sage

CORRESPONDING CRYSTALS: Sapphire, Lapis, Quartz

COLORS: Brown, Gold, Green, Indigo, Orange, Red, Violet, Yellow

SAMHAIN/HALLOWEEN

NORTHERN HEMISPHERE: Oct 31st–Nov 1st
SOUTHERN HEMISPHERE: April 30/May 1st–May 5th
HERBS: Garlic, Sage, Cinnamon
CORRESPONDING CRYSTALS: Obsidian, Smokey Quartz, Onyx
COLORS: Black, Gold, Orange, Red, Silver

"The Sabbats are the eight points at which we connect the inner and the outer cycles: the interstices where the seasonal, the celestial, the communal, the creative, and the personal all meet."
                                                                —Starhawk

How to Work with Crystals for Each of the Sabbats

YULE: Celebrate this time of the night and divine feminine energy. Welcome the power of winter by adding snowflake obsidian to your Yuletide altar. Snowflake obsidian protects you from destructive energies and brings clarity.

IMBOLC: Combine rosemary and amethyst in a dream sachet to enhance your oneiromancy (dream divination) abilities. Dream divination corresponds well with the first awakenings of the earth.

OSTARA: Plant seeds of self-love by utilizing kunzite in a self-care spell. Kunzite helps to remove energy blockages and promotes self-trust.

BELTANE: Emerald is a stone of love and associated with the planet Venus. Venus is the ruling planet of Taurus (one of May's zodiac signs), which makes the emerald a perfect crystal to use during Beltane. Some ways to incorporate emerald into your Beltane festivities include: wearing emerald jewelry, adding it to your prosperity ritual, or representing the element of earth on your ritual pentacle.

LITHA: Carnelian is a stone of passion and vitality. What better way to invite in the beauty of summer than wearing carnelian during your Midsummer celebration? Carnelian will help you express passion, balance your sacral chakra, and improve your communication skills.

LUGHNASAGH: Peridot's power lies in its healing abilities. It calms nervous conditions, opens up the mind, and balances emotions. After the high energy of midsummer, Peridot can help you regulate and ground. Create a spell jar with Peridot so you can keep a little bit of calm with you everywhere you go.

AUTUMN EQUINOX: Lapis Lazuli is a crystal of prosperity, wisdom, and foresight. As we move into the seasons of night, use lapis lazuli to promote enlightenment and knowledge. If you are starting school, or learning something new, keep lapis lazuli close by when studying and doing research to guide your studies.

SAMHAIN: Obsidian is a stone associated with the Greek Underworld, Hades/Pluton. This crystal is helpful for protection and helps you break negative attachments. Use an obsidian mirror for scrying while the veil is thin to connect with the spirit world.

Moon Phases

First
Quarter

Waxing
Crescent

Waxing
Gibbous

Moon
Phases

New
Moon

Full
Moon

Waning
Gibbous

Waning
Crescent

Last
Quarter

The lunar phases have always been a huge part of a Witch's practice. The moon, also known as "Mother Energy," has been used with other elemental forces to amplify spellwork and healing rituals. Like our ever-changing seasons, the moon and its phases have a powerful influence on our physical bodies and emotional and spiritual state. As the moon waxes and wanes, so do our moods and cycles.

Understanding the moon's different phases can equip you with the strong foundational knowledge to harness its beautiful energy while using it in your personal practice. Whether you are a beginner or a seasoned witch, healing crystals and the moon's cyclical changes can help you navigate through these lunar phases and achieve balance in your life. Although many crystals can be well suited for each moon phase, here are a few suggestions to get you started. You can also use the Moon Worksheet on page 163 to help you.

New Moon

The new moon signifies rebirth and new beginnings. An excellent time to manifest your heart's desires. Grab a pen and write down what you are looking to draw into your life under the new moon. Don't forget to include gratitude for what you already have as it is an important step in manifesting. The new moon is also a great time for practicing shadow work, which is uncovering and learning how to correct our hidden toxic patterns in our lives.

LABRADORITE

The stone of transformation and a close relative to the moonstone, this crystal will facilitate changes in your life and enhance the power of manifestation. It beautifully echoes the new moon's darkness with light flashes to remind us of our power even in the darkest times.

Waxing Crescent

During this phase, it's time to be proactive. Working on new projects and initiatives will set the tone for the month to come. As the moon grows bigger and brighter, self-reflection and motivation are key. We have what it takes already within us to achieve what we want.

CITRINE
Citrine will bring forth your creativity while giving you the confidence to achieve your goals. Its high vibrational energy will bring out the sunshine within all of us.

First Quarter

In this phase we want to face head-on what has been holding us back. We can't continue to grow without realizing what we need to overcome. Keep that forward motion and move back into your power with self-awareness.

FLOURITE

A great tool for decision making and focus. Providing clarity into our deeper feelings so we may uncover what we truly want from the heart.

WAXING GIBBOUS

We will feel our progress and momentum pick up during the waxing gibbous. By staying mindful of our intentions, we will start to see things fall into place as they should. Some may begin to feel the intensity of the incoming phase of the Full Moon. Don't be discouraged, as this may be a time to put your faith to the test. Remain patient.

TIGER'S EYE
Known for its good luck and prosperity properties, Tiger's Eye will also block negative energy that could throw you off track from your goals.

FULL MOON

This one can be pretty intense! If you've ever heard the saying, "It must be a full moon," then you already know what we are talking about. Emotions run high during the full moon. We may feel overwhelmed and lack motivation. This is when you want to *release* and let go of what no longer is serving you, whatever that may be. By learning to redirect the moon's abundant energy during this period, we can utilize that power to recharge ourselves and turn over a new leaf.

MOONSTONE

This stone's gentle energy helps to balance us. Particularly women will benefit from this stone's intense feminine energy which will also help men to get in more in touch with their emotions.

Waning Gibbous

It's time to cut ties with anyone or anything that could be toxic in your life. Whether it's friends, bad habits, or emotional connections, it's never selfish and sometimes necessary to want to conserve and protect your own energy. By letting go of these things we can begin to foster the possibilities of new beginnings and opportunities.

SMOKEY QUARTZ

Along with its grounding properties, smokey quartz will assist us in achieving clarity while breaking habits in our life. While we push in a new direction, it will protect us from negative energy while transmuting it into positive energy.

LAST QUARTER

We want to get clear on our goals and intentions in the last quarter and reflect on what is needed to get to where we want to be. For the previous moon phase, we let go of toxic energy surrounding us to clear the way for getting down to business. This is also a time for emotional healing. Is there someone you need to forgive? Maybe it's yourself? If you feel your progress slow down, regroup and remember that slow progress is better than no progress at all.

ROSE QUARTZ

Known as the "Love Stone," Rose Quartz is a warm, loving reminder to give ourselves the self-love we wholeheartedly deserve. A great stone for emotional healing.

Waning Crescent

As the end of the lunar cycle draws near, the waning crescent is a time to surrender and rest. Begin to declutter your mind and or space. If you have kept a journal up to this point, now would be a good time to review and hone in on your journey so far. What can you do to complete this cycle as you prepare for the next?

BLOODSTONE

The purification stone will boost energy and aid in revitalization during this time of much-needed rest.

MOON RITUALS

No matter what phase the moon is in, you can plan a basic ritual to enhance your intentions. Start out by writing down the upcoming dates of the moon phases in your journal. Outline clearly what you would like to work on/manifest/release. Writing down your intentions can help to solidify them.

You can do a moon ritual in a variety of ways. Some may choose to take a bath soak while incorporating crystals, candles, and herbs. Meditating in your sacred space with your crystals. Setting up an altar with crystals to reflect your intent. Outside under the moon is a personal favorite. There is no wrong or right way. This practice should be unique and organic. Let your intuition guide you to what is uniquely you!

A few basic items you will want to collect for your rituals:

- Crystals (Of course!) of any shape or size that correlate to the moon phase
- Moon journal to track your practice
- Sage, Palo Santo, or incense for cleansing your aura prior
- Flowers or Herbs you wish to incorporate into your ritual/spellwork
- Your intention! The magic is within you. (We can't stress that enough)

"The moon does not fight. It attacks no one. It does not worry. It does not try to crush others. It keeps to its course, but by its very nature, it gently influences. What other body could pull an entire ocean from shore to shore? The moon is faithful to its nature and its power is never diminished."

—Deng Ming-Dao

Burning Sage and other sacred herbs (known as smudging) has been used for centuries by ancient cultures including Native Americans. The act of smudging is believed to cleanse your physical and spiritual body (or aura).

Palo Santo "holy wood" comes from a tree grown primarily in South America. Harvested in a sacred manner, these wood sticks are another great choice for cleansing and can be used in tandem with Sage.

4
Crystals in Your Sacred Space

Your sacred space should be your sanctuary. Sometimes, the energy can become stagnant and unpleasant, whether in a room or a small section of your house. Using crystals in your sacred space, can enhance positive energy flow and bring balance to the environment around you. Crystals can be chosen for specific needs and intentions. For example, Rose Quartz is used to channel loving energy into your space. Perhaps you need an extra boost of self-love or would like to create a warm and inviting environment. Rose Quartz would be your go-to!

Sometimes we may focus on how a room looks and it's easy to forget about how a room *feels*. This is where healing crystals for your sacred space come into play. We will be discussing ways to use crystals to enhance and harness their magic while creating an energetically pleasing sacred space.

CRYSTAL ALTARS

The root of the word altar means "A raised structure or place that serves as a center for worship or ritual." Altars have always been significant in spiritual practice throughout history and in different religions such as Catholicism and Buddhism. For centuries, witches have used crystal altars for healing, sabbat offerings, and other magical practices. They are also a perfect setting for your spellwork and can enhance your spells. Some may choose to change their altar on a New or Full moon, by season, monthly or weekly. There are no rules on how long you should keep your altar.

A crystal altar is designed to keep crystal energies flowing and reflects *you* and what aligns with your intention.

Your first altar can be simple and inexpensive to get started. The size of your altar is not important. Initially, you will want to choose where to set up your altar. This should be a tranquil and calm space. Perhaps in a garden, a place where you meditate often, or even on a nightstand or tabletop. Make sure to select a location that will not disturb your setup. If you have small children or pets, you may want to find a place higher up off the ground to keep it safe. Remember to always cleanse the space energetically before setting up a new altar.

Gather any items that resonate with you and your purpose or intention for the altar. Feel free to use materials you already have on hand. Some examples include: pictures, incense, pendulums, precious metals, small trinkets, coins, herbs, totems, flowers, divination tools, statues, feathers, candles, seashells, bells, and objects that represent the four elements, runes and of course crystals!

You will want to select anything that will boost your connection to the universe's energy and that holds significance to you. Whether minimalistic or outlandish, there is no right or wrong way to do this. Rely on your intuition to guide you throughout the process.

If you choose to display the four elements on your altar, a quick guide will help you get started. You can simply represent the elements by collecting items straight from Mother Earth.

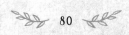

Elements

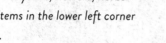

EARTH
Grounding, Stability, Growth
Crystals, flowers, herbs
*Place these items in the lower left corner
of your altar.*

AIR
Intellect, Communication,
Creativity
Feather, bell, incense
Place these items in the upper left corner.

FIRE
Passion, Strong Will,
Inspiration
Candles, matches, pyramid shapes
*Place these items in the lower right corner
of your altar.*

WATER
Emotion, Pleasure, Healing
A vessel containing water,
seashells, driftwood
Place these items in the upper right corner.

If you are short on space or need an alternative to a tabletop altar, try creating a travel-size altar. This should be small enough to fit in a pouch that can be transported with you on vacation or even to your workplace. Another variation would be a hanging altar. Macrame plant holders can be lovely to hold a wooden slab or disc on which you can place your crystals and other small trinkets. Tumbled crystals work best for either of these options.

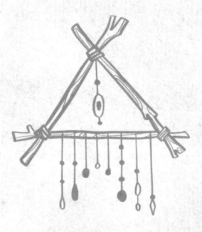

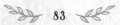

CRYSTALS SUGGESTED FOR ALTAR INTENTIONS

AGATE (BLUE LACE)
CALMING
The soothing blue crystalline layers of this crystal is perfect when looking to achieve a calm and relaxing environment.

AMETHYST
TRANQUILITY
Amethyst helps to keep the mind calm and promotes focus.

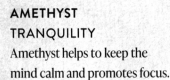

BLOODSTONE
VITALITY
This crystal guards its bearer against physical illness and will promote a vigorous state.

CARNELIAN
CREATIVITY
This stone will boost your creativity and joyous emotions while keeping your feet on the ground when starting a new project.

CITRINE
ABUNDANCE
Also known as the money stone, citrine has been known to attract abundance and prosperity.

FLUORITE
FOCUS
The ultimate crystal for focus, stimulating intellect, concentration, creative inspiration, and decision-making.

ROSE QUARTZ
UNCONDITIONAL LOVE
The stone of love softens the heart and soothes emotions. Its loving energy works wonders.

SMOKEY QUARTZ
PROTECTION
While being nurtured and protected from negative energies, Smokey quartz will also keep you grounded.

CLEAR QUARTZ
CLARITY
We all suffer from brain fog at times and need a little clarity. Let clear quartz provide the mental detox when you need it the most!

TIGER'S EYE
CONFIDENCE
Tiger's eye will give you the courage, strength, and self-confidence to take on anything that comes your way.

Refer to the Crystal quick guide in the back of this book for other crystals and their metaphysical properties.

ANGELITE
AWARENESS
Aligning you with your spiritual truth, Angelite deepens your subconscious awareness.

APOPHYLLITE
MOTIVATION
With the ability to release mental blockages and restore motivation, Apophyllite will keep you determined to complete your task.

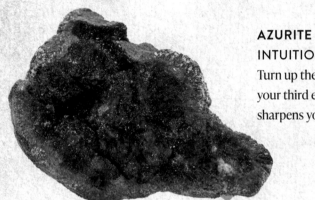

AZURITE
INTUITION

Turn up the volume on
your third eye while Azurite
sharpens your psychic ability.

JADE
LUCK

Highly praised as the stone
of luck, Jade will invite good
fortune into your life.

LABRADORITE
TRANSFORMATION

As "the only constant in life is change," this crystal will gently assist in guiding you towards change for the better.

LEPIDOLITE
PEACE

Lose yourself in the peaceful energy of Lepidolite and its calming influence.

RUBY
PASSION
Use Ruby to ignite your inner flame
while boosting self-confidence

LAPIS
COMMUNICATION
Its deep vibrant blue
correlates to the throat
chakra and is ideal
for facilitating clear
communication.

Building Your Altar

Now that you have selected a safe spot, chosen your crystals, and cleansed your space and crystals, you can start to build your altar! Begin by holding each crystal in your hand before placing them on the altar, and chant a positive affirmation in alignment with your intention. The arrangement and placement are entirely up to you. Repeat this step until you have laid out all your crystals the way you want. Once your crystal placement is complete, please add your other items. Be mindful of your intention while placing each item.

GRIDDING A ROOM

Gridding a room is the act of placing specific crystals in your home to assist in manifesting goals, providing protection, and inviting love, vitality, and abundance. The shape and size of your crystals do not matter while gridding a room. There is no need to break the bank by buying expensive stones either. If you do not have the ones listed below, you can use your intuition to guide you to what stone feels right and suitable for the intention you are setting. Gridding your house or room will boost healing, protecting, and transmuting negative energy.

Step 1: Cleansing

First, you will want to cleanse your space using the methods previously mentioned earlier in the book. There are several reasons you might want to consider cleansing your space. People and events leave an energetic imprint. Through a cleansing ritual, you can remove any stagnant energies left behind and provide a clean slate to set your intentions. Other times to cleanse your space could be after an argument, illness, or death, and provide a fresh start for new endeavors, or if you are feeling a heaviness around you.

Performing a physical cleaning is also recommended to get started! How often should you cleanse your space? Feel free to cleanse your space as often as you feel called to! We typically recommend a thorough cleansing monthly. However, cleansing should be done as often as you feel is necessary!

Step 2: Setting the Intent

Take a moment and think about what it is you want your focus to be before gridding your space. Ask yourself the following:

* What type of energy do you want to invite or cast into your space?
* What feelings do you want to get rid of that no longer serve you?
* What mindset would you love to embody?

There may be many reasons. Feel free to write them down. Once you have your intention clear and concise, you may want to meditate on it to tap into your own energy while visualizing your intent. The act of gridding your space needs to coincide with your mindset. Repeating daily affirmations is an excellent way to do this.

STEP 3: CHOOSING YOUR CRYSTALS

After setting your intention, you can now choose crystals you find best fit this scenario.

ROSE QUARTZ

Bring unconditional love to yourself or a relationship by incorporating Rose Quartz in your home. Its loving vibrations have the energy to replace negative emotions with self-love and confidence. This stone is also wonderful for mending a broken heart. Place this stone in the four corners of your bedroom, under your pillow before bed or on your nightstand.

Chant: "I love myself to the very core of my essence."

TOURMALINE

A powerful and protective stone used to redirect dense or weighted energies into productive and positive energy. Tourmaline should be placed in the outermost corners of the inside or outside of your home. We also suggest keeping a black tourmaline near your electronics to help absorb electromagnetic radiation or electric and magnetic fields.

Chant: "May this home and everyone within be protected at all times."

CITRINE

Citrine is a must if you want to welcome abundance into your life. Historically citrine has been used for success and financial matters. It is one of the most powerful crystals for manifestation. Along with using citrine we want to also practice gratitude for what we already have. This will align our energy with our intention. This crystal should be placed in the far-left corner of your home from your front door, also known as the "wealth corner."

Chant: "I am deserving of wealth and abundance in my life."

SELENITE

Selenite is fabulous for bringing balance and cleansing into our lives by warding off unwanted energies and outside forces. This beautiful translucid crystal is perfect for keeping in any room to promote a peaceful atmosphere. You may like to use it is over doorways or on top of door frames to cleanse the energy coming in and out of your house. Small rod or wand- like formations are best for this spot as it is inconspicuous. Windowsills are another great option.

Always make sure not to get selenite wet since it is a soft mineral and will disintegrate when it comes into contact with liquids.

Chant: "May this house be filled with bright light and positivity."

CLEAR QUARTZ

Using clear quartz in your home can be both pleasing to your decor and your energetic alignment. A distinctive property of clear quartz is the ability to clear/wash/purify the energy around it, making it a wonderful crystal to use in the home. You can freely place a clear quartz anywhere you feel the need to. Trust your intuition on this.

Chant: "This space is purified and positive energy flows throughout."

AMETHYST

Amethyst, a purple variety of quartz, is known to help calm and sooth emotions and enhance awareness while guiding us to reach higher states of consciousness. This stone is your remedy if you are dealing with stress or grief. It is also wonderful when paired with selenite. For those who deal with lack of sleep or trouble falling asleep, keep Amethyst at your bedside to enhance a restful night's sleep.

Chant: "I am calm and trust my intuition."

CRYSTAL GRIDS

Crystal grids use symbols of sacred geometry to amplify the energy of our intention. Like an altar, specific crystals are chosen based on the goal of your grid and are used to supercharge your desired result. Think of them as a vibrational blueprint capable of changing the energetic vibration of you and your space.

Crystal grids can be used for self-healing or to send out positive vibrations to others. They balance the energy in high traffic zones which makes them ideal for your desk at work or any other frequently occupied space.

Crystals laid out in a geometric arrangement help direct the energy flow to your intention. The Seed Of Life and the Flower Of Life are two commonly used geometric grids. These patterns serve as energetic visuals with a spiritual meaning associated with them. There are many resources online for printable grids to help get you started. Although a physical copy of a sacred design is not essential for gridding, it is encouraged to have a basic understanding of the different patterns and how they will aid in your energy work.

Some common uses for crystal grids include:

- Manifesting
- Self-healing
- Distance healing
- Protection
- Spiritual well being
- Charging and activating crystals
- Positive energy flow in the home
- Balancing the energy of your space
- Conquering fear
- Controlling emotions
- Building courage
- Healing a broken heart
- House blessing

Sacred Geometric Grids and How You Can Use Them:

Flower of Life

"THE UNIVERSE"

"The master of sacred geometry" represents the cycle of creation. This powerful shape has nineteen overlapping circles of equal proportion that are interconnected. The circle in the middle of the shape depicts how all life comes from one source. Some believe that this shape holds the secrets and patterns of our magical universe. Often used in conjunction with Reiki healing, this shape is all-purpose and can create a calm and soothing environment.

CRYSTAL SUGGESTIONS: Selenite, Tourmaline, Green Aventurine

Seed of Life

"CREATION"

Comprised of seven overlapping circles, the Seed of Life symbolizes creation. In sacred geometry, circles represent cycles. Seeds are the basis for life, and this grid will serve as a reminder of the flow of energy through the universe. This shape is ideal to use during a period of transformation and new beginnings.

CRYSTAL SUGGESTIONS: Labradorite, Lapis Lazuli, Clear Quartz

Metatron's Cube

"SPIRITUALITY"

This shape's name originates from the archangel Metatron, the angel of life. It is a distinct pattern that symbolizes the underlying patterns of the universe and is said to contain all the shapes and patterns that exist in the universe. It is also believed that the circles of Metatron's cube symbolize the feminine, while the straight lines represent the masculine. When needing balance and harmony, the Metatron's cube is your go-to for crystal gridding.

CRYSTAL SUGGESTIONS: Rutilated Quartz, Selenite, Angelite, Celestite

SRI YANTRA

"CLARITY"

The Sri Yantra originated in Hinduism and is the symbol for gods and goddesses in the Hindu culture. It consists of nine interlocking triangles. In addition to its beautiful and intricate structure, this shape does wonders for meditation. While possessing a source of supreme energy, this grid is excellent for bringing enlightenment and mental stability.

CRYSTAL SUGGESTIONS: Rose quartz, Clear Quartz, Selenite

Infinite Hexagram

"BALANCE"

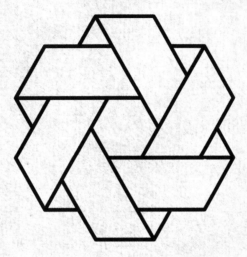

With three sets of six-pointed hexagrams enclosed by a circle, this grid helps to restore energetic order while supporting growth and change. A powerful grid to rejuvenate the body, mind, and spirit. It is often used to connect with multi-dimensions of consciousness.

CRYSTAL SUGGESTIONS: Moldavite, Libyan Desert Glass, Hematite, Clear Quartz

SUNBURST

"REJUVENATE"

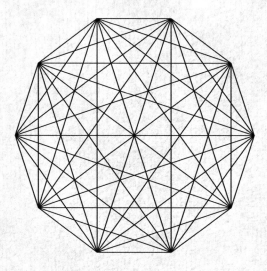

Just like the bright rays of our sun, the Sunburst radiates positive energy. It is highly revitalizing and can help balance all the chakras using correlating crystals. An excellent choice when working with distant healing and Reiki.

CRYSTAL SUGGESTIONS: Sunstone, Citrine, Carnelian

> There are many different grid options to choose from online or at your local crystal shop. Grid cloths are a versatile option as they can be folded up neatly and transported discreetly.

MERKABA

"STABILITY"

If you break down the word Merkaba: Mer means Light, Ka means Spirit, Ba means Body. As a geometric shape of the human energy field, the Merkaba symbol consists of two intersecting tetrahedrons, one pointing down and the other pointing up. This shape acts as a spiritual activator and is used when seeking balance, power, protection, and spiritual enlightenment.

CRYSTAL SUGGESTIONS: Amethyst, Clear Quartz, Fluorite

It is entirely up to you if you prefer to do this freeform. Basic mandala designs or anything with symmetry is a great option when first starting out A simple yet effective grid can be comprised of five crystals. One crystal represents each cardinal direction: North, South, East, and West. Quartz points are recommended to direct the energy; however, you can use similar stones that appeal to you. Your center crystal is your master crystal. This is the crystal that represents the intention for your grid. Be sure to hone in on the focus for your grid.

CREATING YOUR GRID

You will take the steps mentioned in Crystal Altars before setting up your grid. Feel free to also use the Crystal Grid worksheet on page 162.

STEP 1: CLEANSING YOUR SPACE—You always want to clear out dense energy before starting something new.

STEP 2: SET YOUR INTENTION—Write your intention on paper and display it in the center of your grid, or keep it in your thoughts.

STEP 3: CHOOSING AND PROGRAMMING YOUR CRYSTALS—Your selection can be intuitively chosen, or you may want to research crystals that best support your purpose.

Once you have performed the three steps above, you are now ready to set up your crystal grid.

While keeping your intention in the forefront of your mind, first begin with the outer crystals. You will work your way to the center and place your master crystal last. Now you will want to activate your grid. You can do this by using your finger or a quartz crystal and tracing a line from each crystal on the grid as if you are connecting the dots. Another way to do this is to sit quietly and meditate while visualizing your intentions.

TIPS

- Your grid should be constructed somewhere it is not easily disturbed. You will want to keep your grid in tact anywhere from a few days to a few weeks. Go with your gut on this. You will know when it is time to deconstruct it.

- Another way to utilize crystals in your sacred space is to place them in or around your house plants either on top of the soil or near the roots. Your plants will keep the crystals supercharged due to their grounding nature and the crystals will encourage the overall health of the plant. Moss agate, known as the gardener's stone, will work wonders with any plant or garden. Other crystals that work well in vegetation are Moonstone, Citrine, Calcite, Clear Quartz and Tiger's eye.

5
CRYSTALS IN SPELLWORK

Crystals serve as a powerful magical conduit in spellwork. They can be added to any spell already tucked away in your arsenal or for one you have yet to create! As we know, crystals amplify the energy of what is around and have their own energy field. This makes them versatile in use for any spell or intention.

Using crystals in spellwork is not limiting, and the more you study their magical properties, the more comfortable you will be in getting creative with them! Clear quartz is a great place to start, as this crystal is much like rosemary as an herb; it can be used as a substitute for any crystal and will not hinder your spell work or negate your intentions in any way.

One of the most commonly cast spells is a spell to banish troublesome entities or release energy weighing us down.

A creative way that I used crystals for a spell was when I was asked to banish a parasitic entity that was leeching off of someone's energy. I drew up my pentacle with sigils, blessed my candle, and gathered two clear quartz crystals. Clear quartz is one of my favorites to work with because of its versatility and power to amplify. I placed a clear male crystal in the top right corner above my pentacle, and a cloudy female crystal at the top left. My intuition told me the balance of divine masculine and feminine energy would be needed in this spell.

> **SIGIL:** Sigil comes from the word "sigillum" which means "seal," "sign," and "character." Similar in definition to the Greek word "gramma", and the proto-Germanic word "runir". Sigils are signs and seals used to amplify magic through the power of the written word. You can create a sigil from any letters or characters, or develop your own signs.

Sometimes we are called to certain configurations and setups even though we have not previously read about them or heard about them; follow your well-trained intuition regarding spellwork. Symbolism is important, and we must study our correspondences, but once we have this knowledge, we can expand our own creativity. The clear quartz worked especially well for my banishment spell, and I would use that technique again, and recommend to others. Feel free to incorporate this technique, and to then make it your own.

Reminder–Always draw a circle when calling in deities, casting banishing spells, or any spell you feel you will need protection. When in doubt, draw a circle.

What are "male" and "female" crystals?

As known in crystal grid work, there are "male" and "female" crystals, and each is used in its appropriate resonance as part of a crystal grid. Male crystals are mostly, if not completely, clear and you can easily see through them. Female crystals are cloudy in nature and often look like frosted glass. When we mention "male" and "female" we speak of the divine masculine and feminine correspondences.

Blessing a Crystal for Healing

SUPPLIES

- Labradorite
- Lighter
- White candle or tea light
- Healing sigil
- Full moon water (optional)

First, create a healing sigil by using Witches' Wheel or your own symbols or letters. Then, inscribe this sigil onto the tealight using a pin or thumbtack, and put it to the side for later. If you choose to incorporate moon water, pour about a cup of water into a bowl and perform a blessing by drawing a pentacle in the air over the bowl and imagining the pentacle glowing electric blue.

Repeat these words: "I bless this moon water with healing energy. May this water cleanse my crystal and amplify its healing properties." Now, set your blessed water on the west side of your east-facing altar. You are ready to begin the spell.

Take your labradorite and place it in your bowl of water. You may repeat, "I place my crystal in this blessed water to be cleansed and charged with healing energy," or adapt with another incantation of your own. Now that the crystal has been cleansed by water, you will cleanse it by fire. Draw a pentacle in the air over your candle, trace the lines of the sigil, and imagine the lines glowing red like embers while repeating, "I charge this sigil and activate its healing properties. May this sigil charge my crystal and amplify its healing properties."

Once your sigil is charged, you may light the candle and hold the crystal (safely) over the flame. Notice how the energy flows, and the energy your crystal gives off while being charged. You may now place your crystal near the candle and let the candle burn all the way through.

REMINDER: Never leave a candle burning unattended. It is okay to snuff out a candle and relight it another day to continue the energy work.

SPELLS

The following spells are intended for both beginner and seasoned witches. You may add to them as you see fit through your practice to create unique magic of your own. When spell casting, your intent is as vital to your success as are your beliefs. Make sure to get clear on your intention. Visualization is also a key component. When you start out, create a quiet space for yourself to help you reflect and focus on your practice. Use the Spell Worksheet template on page 164 to help you cast spells.

DREAM SPELL

Dreamwork takes practice and deep inner exploration. As you begin to tune into your subconscious mind and learn to interpret your dreams, a simple dream spell can assist you.

SUPPLIES

- Dried Mugwort
- Bay Laurel
- Lavender
- Crystals: Amethyst

Affirmation: "I am becoming more aware of the messages in my dreams"

1 Draw yourself a bath and add the herbs and amethyst to the water. As you soak, fill yourself with the intentions of dreaming and recalling those dreams.

2 Envision a specific dream you would like to call in or allow your higher knowledge to be expressed in your dream state.

3 Once finished with the bath, take the amethyst and place it under your pillow.

4 Keep a journal on your nightstand to write down any dreams that occurred during the night.

VITALITY SPELL

A wonderful way to boost your healing process or remain in good health is to cast a vitality spell. This can be done for yourself or for family and friends so that you wish wellness upon them. Tailor this spell to the ailment specifically needing attention, whether emotional or physical.

1 Light your candle.

2 Place the rosemary, bay leaf, mint, salt, and crystal inside the jar in whichever order you choose.

3 Close the jar and pour a small amount of wax on the top. Press your thumbprint into the wax (if the vitality spell is meant for yourself).

4 Keep your spell jar nearby or hold it when you feel the need for healing. You can also use a pouch or sachet for this spell if you wish to carry it and omit sealing it with wax. When casting for others, you may create the like and gift it to them.

Affirmation: "I am ready to embrace good health."

SUPPLIES

- A small jar with a lid
- White candle
- Matches or lighter
- Salt
- Rosemary
- Bay leaf
- Mint
- Crystals: Bloodstone

PROTECTION SPELL

Feeling unsafe can drain your energy and make you feel vulnerable to negative forces around you. By protecting your energy, you can act and think clearly. This spell can be cast anywhere and anytime you feel the need to increase your dynamic defenses.

SUPPLIES

- Crystals: Tourmaline

1 Take a few deep inhales and exhales to relax your body.

2 Begin to visualize a personal energy shield around your entire body comprised of mirrors with the reflective side facing out. This will deflect the negative energy away from you.

3 Set the intention to only let in positivity and love.

4 Carry tourmaline in your pocket to amplify the protective vibrations. If mirrors do not resonate with you, you can also visualize any type of impermeable barrier around yourself. Some may also call in their spirit animal to guard them.

Affirmation: "I am divinely protected in all I do."

SELF-LOVE SPELL

Practicing self-love will help everything else in your life fall into place. This mindset will raise your personal vibration and attract what you truly desire.

1 Write on your paper positive affirmations about yourself or what you would like to work on regarding self-love.

2 Sprinkle your rose petals and lavender on the piece of paper, then fold it neatly to ensure the herbs do not spill out. Wrap the string around it to secure it in place.

3 Light your candle and begin to meditate on your intention while holding your crystal in your palm. If you choose to lie down, you can place it on your heart chakra.

4 After you are done, blow out your candle, then set your crystal on top of your paper safely. Feel free to repeat as often as you feel necessary.

Affirmation: "Being myself is enough."
REMINDER: Never leave a candle burning unattended. It is okay to snuff out a candle and relight it another day to continue the energy work.

SUPPLIES

- Pen and paper
- Pink or Red candle
- Matches or a lighter
- String
- Rose Petals
- Lavender
- Crystals: Rose Quartz or Kunzite

"Whether in the ocean, a pebble, a gemstone, or yourself, the energy of the universe permeates all."
—Sarah Bartlett

PROSPERITY SPELL

Whether you are looking to bolster your luck or have a specific intent in mind, a prosperity spell can attract good fortune your way. The universe acts in vibrations and repetition. To attract prosperity, you must also show gratitude for what you already have and believe what you are manifesting is already yours.

SUPPLIES

- Pen and Paper
- Green candle
- Matches or lighter
- A glass of drinking water
- Crystals: Citrine

1 Take your citrine and place it in your glass of water. The duration of how long to infuse your water is entirely up to you. You can leave it for a few minutes or even overnight.

2 On your paper, summarize in one word what you are manifesting in your life regarding prosperity.

3 Light your candle and take a few moments to visualize and meditate on what you wrote down. Feel it as though it is already yours.

4 Remove the citrine from your glass and drink the infused water.

5 Carry your citrine with you and continue to visualize your intention daily.

Affirmation: "I am grateful for all that I have and all that is coming to me."

AURA-CLEANSING SPELL

Over time your aura can become unbalanced due to stresses in your everyday life. This spell can clear negative energy surrounding your aura and bring you back into energetic alignment.

1 Make a list on your paper of the negativity in your life that you want to release on your paper. This can include feelings towards a person, a place, emotions, or any situation that is no longer serving you.

2 Light your sage bundle and proceed to cleanse yourself as you would an object.

3 Take your selenite crystal and run it from head to toe starting at your crown chakra (slightly above your head) and working your way down through all your chakras to your root. This may be repeated as you feel necessary.

4 Light your candle. While staring into the flame, take three deep breaths in and release them. Imagine all that you are releasing starting to rise from your body, falling away from you, and dissipating with your mind's eye. Keep breathing while doing this until you feel lighter and centered.

5 Once you are done, burn your piece of paper in a fire-safe dish.

Affirmation: "I am now clear of any and all energy that no longer serves me."

SUPPLIES

- Pen and Paper
- White Candle
- Matches or lighter
- Sage Bundle
- Fire-safe dish
- Crystals: Selenite

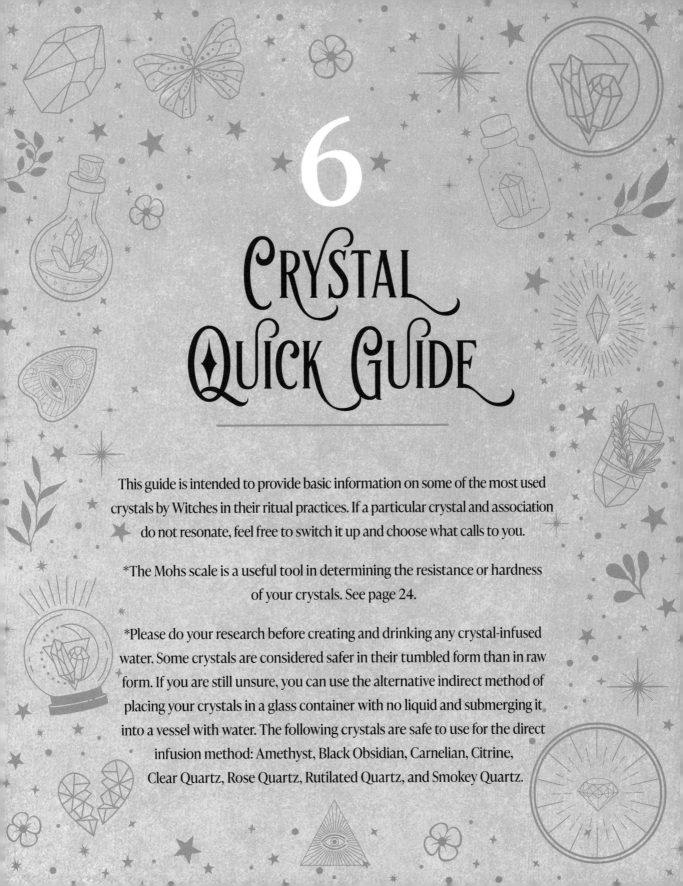

6

CRYSTAL QUICK GUIDE

This guide is intended to provide basic information on some of the most used crystals by Witches in their ritual practices. If a particular crystal and association do not resonate, feel free to switch it up and choose what calls to you.

*The Mohs scale is a useful tool in determining the resistance or hardness of your crystals. See page 24.

*Please do your research before creating and drinking any crystal-infused water. Some crystals are considered safer in their tumbled form than in raw form. If you are still unsure, you can use the alternative indirect method of placing your crystals in a glass container with no liquid and submerging it into a vessel with water. The following crystals are safe to use for the direct infusion method: Amethyst, Black Obsidian, Carnelian, Citrine, Clear Quartz, Rose Quartz, Rutilated Quartz, and Smokey Quartz.

Amethyst

ELEMENT: Air
PLANET: Uranus
HARDNESS: 7
WATER SAFE: Yes
ZODIAC: Aquarius
CHAKRA: Third Eye, Crown
METAPHYSICAL PROPERTIES:
Wisdom, Intuition, Calming

Apophyllite

ELEMENT: Air
PLANET: Venus
HARDNESS: 7
WATER SAFE: No
ZODIAC: Libra
CHAKRA: Third Eye
METAPHYSICAL PROPERTIES:
Recovery, Vitality, Spirituality

Amazonite

ELEMENT: Air
PLANET: Mercury
HARDNESS: 6–6.5
WATER SAFE: Yes
ZODIAC: Gemini, Virgo
CHAKRA: Throat
METAPHYSICAL PROPERTIES:
Courage, Communication, Balance

Agate

ELEMENT: Fire
PLANET: Jupiter
HARDNESS: 6.5–7
WATER SAFE: Yes
ZODIAC: Gemini
CHAKRA: All
METAPHYSICAL PROPERTIES:
Grounding, Harmony, Confidence

APATITE

ELEMENT: Earth
PLANET: Mercury
HARDNESS: 5
WATER SAFE: Yes
ZODIAC: Virgo
CHAKRA: Throat
METAPHYSICAL PROPERTIES:
Communication, Motivation,
Self-Acceptance

AQUAMARINE

ELEMENT: Air, Water
PLANET: Uranus
HARDNESS: 7.5–8
WATER SAFE: Yes
ZODIAC: Aquarius, Pisces
CHAKRA: Throat
METAPHYSICAL PROPERTIES:
Happiness, Calming, Inner Strength

Amber

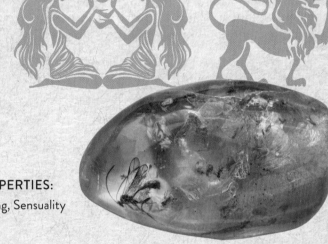

ELEMENT: Fire, Water
PLANET: Mercury, Sun
HARDNESS: 2–2.5
WATER SAFE: Yes
ZODIAC: Gemini, Leo
CHAKRA: Solar Plexus
METAPHYSICAL PROPERTIES:
Courage, Psychic Shielding, Sensuality

Angelite

ELEMENT: Air, Water
PLANET: Neptune, Uranus
HARDNESS: 3.5
WATER SAFE: No
ZODIAC: Aquarius, Pisces
CHAKRA: Throat
METAPHYSICAL PROPERTIES:
Divine Connection,
Communication, Calming

Aventurine

ELEMENT: Earth, Water
PLANET: Earth, Neptune
HARDNESS: 6.5–7
WATER SAFE: Yes
ZODIAC: Capricorn, Pisces
CHAKRA: Heart
METAPHYSICAL PROPERTIES:
Prosperity, Joy, Abundance

Aragonite

ELEMENT: Water
PLANET: Pisces
HARDNESS: 3.5–4
WATER SAFE: No
ZODIAC: Pisces
CHAKRA: Sacral
METAPHYSICAL PROPERTIES:
Creativity, Energy, Stability

BLOODSTONE

ELEMENT: Water
PLANET: Moon
HARDNESS: 6.5–7
WATER SAFE: Yes
ZODIAC: Cancer
CHAKRA: Sacral, Root
METAPHYSICAL PROPERTIES:
Motivation, Strength, Resilience

BISMUTH

ELEMENT: Earth
PLANET: Venus
HARDNESS: 2–2.5
WATER SAFE: No
ZODIAC: Taurus
CHAKRA: All
METAPHYSICAL PROPERTIES:
Transformation, Focus, Courage

Black Moonstone

ELEMENT: Water
PLANET: Moon
HARDNESS: 6–6.5
WATER SAFE: Yes
ZODIAC: Cancer
CHAKRA: Crown
METAPHYSICAL PROPERTIES:
Fertility, Protection, Hope

Calcite

ELEMENT: Water
PLANET: Moon
HARDNESS: 3
WATER SAFE: Yes
ZODIAC: Aries, Cancer
CHAKRA: Crown, Third Eye, Solar Plexus
METAPHYSICAL PROPERTIES:
Clarity, Purifying, Healing

Carnelian

ELEMENT: Fire
PLANET: Mars, Sun
HARDNESS: 6–7
WATER SAFE: Yes
ZODIAC: Leo, Virgo
CHAKRA: Sacral
METAPHYSICAL PROPERTIES:
Creativity, Motivation, Confidence

Citrine

ELEMENT: Fire
PLANET: Sun
HARDNESS: 7
WATER SAFE: Yes
ZODIAC: Leo
CHAKRA: Solar Plexus
METAPHYSICAL PROPERTIES:
Confidence, Abundance, Happiness

Celestite

ELEMENT: Water
PLANET: Neptune, Venus
HARDNESS: 3–3.5
WATER SAFE: No
ZODIAC: Libra
CHAKRA: Third Eye, Crown
METAPHYSICAL PROPERTIES:
Higher Consciousness, Wisdom,
Dream Enhancement

Charoite

ELEMENT: Water
PLANET: Neptune, Pluto
HARDNESS: 5–6
WATER SAFE: Yes
ZODIAC: Aquarius
CHAKRA: Crown, Third Eye
METAPHYSICAL PROPERTIES:
Intuition, Spiritual Transformation,
Divine Guidance

Chrysocolla

ELEMENT: Earth
PLANET: Earth
HARDNESS: 2.5–3.5
WATER SAFE: No
ZODIAC: Libra
CHAKRA: Throat, Heart
METAPHYSICAL PROPERTIES:
Unconditional Love, Enhances Personal
Power, Communication

Chalcedony

ELEMENT: Water
PLANET: Venus
HARDNESS: 6–7
WATER SAFE: Yes
ZODIAC: Aquarius, Libra
CHAKRA: Crown, Third Eye, Throat
METAPHYSICAL PROPERTIES:
Calming, Compassion, Balance

CHRYSOPRASE

ELEMENT: Water
PLANET: Neptune
HARDNESS: 6–7
WATER SAFE: Yes
ZODIAC: Pisces
CHAKRA: Heart
METAPHYSICAL PROPERTIES:
Self Esteem, Confidence, Self-Love

COPPER

ELEMENT: Air
PLANET: Venus
HARDNESS: 3
WATER SAFE: Yes
ZODIAC: Gemini, Scorpio
CHAKRA: Solar Plexus, Sacral
METAPHYSICAL PROPERTIES:
Grounding, Desire, Energy Conduit

Danburite

ELEMENT: Air
PLANET: Venus
HARDNESS: 6
WATER SAFE: Yes
ZODIAC: Libra
CHAKRA: Crown, Third Eye, Heart
METAPHYSICAL PROPERTIES:
Harmony, Happiness, Calming

Diamond

ELEMENT: Earth
PLANET: Venus
HARDNESS: 10
WATER SAFE: Yes
ZODIAC: Aries
CHAKRA: Crown
METAPHYSICAL PROPERTIES:
Fearlessness, Fortitude, Inner Power

DIOPTASE

ELEMENT: Earth
PLANET: Venus, Saturn
HARDNESS: 5
WATER SAFE: No
ZODIAC: Capricorn, Virgo
CHAKRA: Heart
METAPHYSICAL PROPERTIES:
Love, Forgiveness, Compassion

DUMORTIERITE

ELEMENT: Earth
PLANET: Jupiter
HARDNESS: 7–8.5
WATER SAFE: Yes
ZODIAC: Sagittarius
CHAKRA: Throat, Third Eye
METAPHYSICAL PROPERTIES:
Harmony, Peace, Intuition

Emerald

ELEMENT: Water
PLANET: Venus
HARDNESS: 7.5–8
WATER SAFE: Yes
ZODIAC: Taurus, Gemini
CHAKRA: Heart
METAPHYSICAL PROPERTIES:
Success, Wisdom, Love

Epidote

ELEMENT: Air
PLANET: Mercury
HARDNESS: 6–7
WATER SAFE: Yes
ZODIAC: Capricorn
CHAKRA: Heart
METAPHYSICAL PROPERTIES:
Spiritual Growth, Dream Enhancement, Healing

Fluorite

ELEMENT: Water
PLANET: Mercury
HARDNESS: 4
WATER SAFE: No
ZODIAC: Gemini, Aquarius
CHAKRA: Crown, Third Eye
METAPHYSICAL PROPERTIES:
Focus, Decision Making, Insight

Fuchsite

ELEMENT: Water and Air
PLANET: Venus
HARDNESS: 2–3
WATER SAFE: No
ZODIAC: Libra
CHAKRA: Throat, Heart
METAPHYSICAL PROPERTIES:
Healing, Balance, Detoxification

GALENA

ELEMENT: Air
PLANET: Uranus
HARDNESS: 2.5
WATER SAFE: No
ZODIAC: Aquarius
CHAKRA: Root
METAPHYSICAL PROPERTIES:
Compassion, Love, Harmony

GARNET

ELEMENT: Fire
PLANET: Mars
HARDNESS: 6.5–7.5
WATER SAFE: No
ZODIAC: Aries
CHAKRA: Root
METAPHYSICAL PROPERTIES:
Revitalizing, Passion, Devotion

Goldstone

ELEMENT: Air, Earth
PLANET: Venus
HARDNESS: 5–6
WATER SAFE: Yes
ZODIAC: Taurus
CHAKRA: Third Eye
METAPHYSICAL PROPERTIES:
Stability, Courage, Confidence

Hematite

ELEMENT: Earth
PLANET: Earth, Mars
HARDNESS: 5.5–6.5
WATER SAFE: No
ZODIAC: Taurus, Capricorn
CHAKRA: Root
METAPHYSICAL PROPERTIES:
Grounding, Protection, Balance

HOWLITE

ELEMENT: Water
PLANET: Moon
HARDNESS: 2.5–3.5
WATER SAFE: Yes
ZODIAC: Cancer
CHAKRA: Crown
METAPHYSICAL PROPERTIES:
Calming, Purity, Cleansing

IOLITE

ELEMENT: Earth
PLANET: Mercury
HARDNESS: 7–7.5
WATER SAFE: No
ZODIAC: Virgo
CHAKRA: Third Eye
METAPHYSICAL PROPERTIES:
Intuition, Communication, Intellect

Jade

ELEMENT: Air
PLANET: Jupiter
HARDNESS: 6–6.5
WATER SAFE: Yes
ZODIAC: Libra
CHAKRA: Heart
METAPHYSICAL PROPERTIES:
Good Luck, Prosperity, Positivity

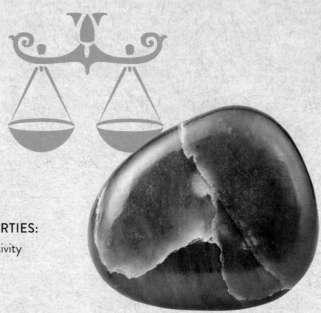

Kunzite

ELEMENT: Air
PLANET: Venus
HARDNESS: 6–7.5
WATER SAFE: No
ZODIAC: Taurus, Libra
CHAKRA: Heart
METAPHYSICAL PROPERTIES:
Self Love, Compassion, Well Being

Kyanite

ELEMENT: Earth
PLANET: Earth
HARDNESS: 4–7
WATER SAFE: No
ZODIAC: Virgo, Aquarius, Pisces
CHAKRA: Throat
METAPHYSICAL PROPERTIES:
Balance, Relaxation, Wisdom

Lapis Lazuli

ELEMENT: Fire
PLANET: Jupiter
HARDNESS: 5–6
WATER SAFE: No
ZODIAC: Sagittarius
CHAKRA: Throat
METAPHYSICAL PROPERTIES:
Communication, Honesty, Wisdom

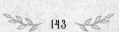

LABRADORITE

ELEMENT: Water
PLANET: Neptune
HARDNESS: 6–6.5
WATER SAFE: No
ZODIAC: Pisces
CHAKRA: Third Eye, Crown
METAPHYSICAL PROPERTIES:
Transformation, Reflection, Loyalty

LEPIDOLITE

ELEMENT: Water
PLANET: Neptune
HARDNESS: 2.5–3
WATER SAFE: No
ZODIAC: Pisces
CHAKRA: Crown, Third Eye
METAPHYSICAL PROPERTIES:
Uplifting, Calming, Awareness

Malachite

ELEMENT: Earth
PLANET: Venus
HARDNESS: 3.5–4
WATER SAFE: No
ZODIAC: Capricorn
CHAKRA: Heart
METAPHYSICAL PROPERTIES:
Empathy, Growth, Love

Moonstone

ELEMENT: Water
PLANET: Moon
HARDNESS: 6.5
WATER SAFE: Yes
ZODIAC: Gemini
CHAKRA: Third Eye
METAPHYSICAL PROPERTIES:
Fertility, Intuition, Spiritual Purity

MOLDAVITE

ELEMENT: Fire
PLANET: All
HARDNESS: 6.5–7
WATER SAFE: No
ZODIAC: All
CHAKRA: Heart
METAPHYSICAL PROPERTIES:
Transformation, Psychic Abilities,
Awareness

MOOKAITE

ELEMENT: Earth
PLANET: Earth
HARDNESS: 7
WATER SAFE: No
ZODIAC: Virgo, Scorpio
CHAKRA: Solar Plexus, Root
METAPHYSICAL PROPERTIES:
Strength, Courage, Vitality

◊ OBSIDIAN

ELEMENT: Fire
PLANET: Venus, Pluto
HARDNESS: 5–5.5
WATER SAFE: Yes
ZODIAC: Scorpio
CHAKRA: Root
METAPHYSICAL PROPERTIES:
Protection, Grounding, Shielding

◊ ONYX

ELEMENT: Earth
PLANET: Pluto
HARDNESS: 6–7
WATER SAFE: Yes
ZODIAC: Capricorn
CHAKRA: Root
METAPHYSICAL PROPERTIES:
Willpower, Focus, Protection

Opal

ELEMENT: Water
PLANET: Saturn
HARDNESS: 5.5–6
WATER SAFE: Yes
ZODIAC: Pisces, Libra
CHAKRA: All
METAPHYSICAL PROPERTIES:
Memory Retention, Purity, Faith

Pietersite

ELEMENT: Fire
PLANET: Jupiter
HARDNESS: 5–6
WATER SAFE: No
ZODIAC: Gemini, Virgo
CHAKRA: Root, Solar Plexus
METAPHYSICAL PROPERTIES:
Personal Power, Self-Discovery, Energy

PERIDOT

ELEMENT: Fire
PLANET: Pluto
HARDNESS: 6.5–7
WATER SAFE: Yes
ZODIAC: Leo
CHAKRA: Heart
METAPHYSICAL PROPERTIES:
Vitality, Strength, Abundance

PREHNITE

ELEMENT: Earth
PLANET: Earth
HARDNESS: 6–6.5
WATER SAFE: No
ZODIAC: Virgo, Capricorn
CHAKRA: Heart
METAPHYSICAL PROPERTIES:
Unconditional Love, Precognition,
Angelic Connection

Pyrite

ELEMENT: Fire
PLANET: Sun
HARDNESS: 6.5–7
WATER SAFE: No
ZODIAC: Leo
CHAKRA: Solar Plexus, Sacral, Root
METAPHYSICAL PROPERTIES:
Confidence, Protection, Abundance

Quartz: Clear

ELEMENT: All
PLANET: All
HARDNESS: 7
WATER SAFE: Yes
ZODIAC: All
CHAKRA: All
METAPHYSICAL PROPERTIES:
Clarity, Purify, Cleanse

Quartz: Rose

ELEMENT: Water
PLANET: Venus
HARDNESS: 7
WATER SAFE: Yes
ZODIAC: Taurus, Libra
CHAKRA: Heart
METAPHYSICAL PROPERTIES: Love,
Compassion, Empathy

Quartz: Smokey

ELEMENT: Earth
PLANET: Pluto
HARDNESS: 7
WATER SAFE: Yes
ZODIAC: Scorpio
CHAKRA: Root
METAPHYSICAL PROPERTIES:
Protection, Grounding, Stability

Quartz: Rutilated

ELEMENT: Fire
PLANET: Venus
HARDNESS: 7
WATER SAFE: Yes
ZODIAC: Leo
CHAKRA: Solar Plexus, Sacral, Root
METAPHYSICAL PROPERTIES:
Energy, Concentration, Spiritual Growth

Rhodonite

ELEMENT: Earth
PLANET: Venus
HARDNESS: 5.5–6.5
WATER SAFE: Yes
ZODIAC: Capricorn, Libra
CHAKRA: Heart
METAPHYSICAL PROPERTIES:
Love, Self-Worth, Wellbeing

Rhodochrosite

ELEMENT: Water
PLANET: Venus
HARDNESS: 3.5–4
WATER SAFE: No
ZODIAC: Libra
CHAKRA: Heart
METAPHYSICAL PROPERTIES:
Calming, Love, Passion

Ruby

ELEMENT: Fire
PLANET: Mars
HARDNESS: 9
WATER SAFE: Yes
ZODIAC: Aries, Leo
CHAKRA: Root
METAPHYSICAL PROPERTIES:
Concentration, Fearlessness, Passion

Shungite

ELEMENT: Earth
PLANET: Mercury
HARDNESS: 3.5
WATER SAFE: Yes
ZODIAC: Capricorn, Scorpio
CHAKRA: Root
METAPHYSICAL PROPERTIES:
Grounding, EMF Shielding, Purifying

Sapphire

ELEMENT: Air
PLANET: Mercury
HARDNESS: 9
WATER SAFE: Yes
ZODIAC: Virgo, Leo
CHAKRA: Crown, Third Eye
METAPHYSICAL PROPERTIES:
Concentration, Abundance, Wisdom

SELENITE

ELEMENT: Water
PLANET: Moon
HARDNESS: 2
WATER SAFE: No
ZODIAC: Cancer
CHAKRA: Crown
METAPHYSICAL PROPERTIES:
Clarity, Positivity, Purification

SODALITE

ELEMENT: Earth
PLANET: Jupiter
HARDNESS: 5.5–6
WATER SAFE: Yes
ZODIAC: Sagittarius
CHAKRA: Throat
METAPHYSICAL PROPERTIES:
Communication, Harmony, Self-Trust

Sunstone

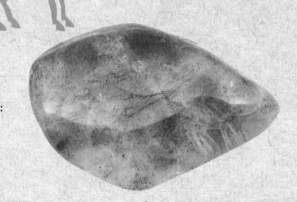

ELEMENT: Fire
PLANET: Mars
HARDNESS: 6–6.5
WATER SAFE: Yes
ZODIAC: Aries
CHAKRA: Solar Plexus
METAPHYSICAL PROPERTIES:
Uplifting, Positivity, Confidence

Tiger's Eye

ELEMENT: Fire
PLANET: Sun
HARDNESS: 7
WATER SAFE: Yes
ZODIAC: Leo
CHAKRA: Solar Plexus
METAPHYSICAL PROPERTIES:
Confidence, Courage, Fortune

Topaz

ELEMENT: Air
PLANET: Mercury, Jupiter
HARDNESS: 8
WATER SAFE: No
ZODIAC: Virgo
CHAKRA: Third Eye, Throat
METAPHYSICAL PROPERTIES:
Self Realization, Peace, Calming

Tourmaline

ELEMENT: Water
PLANET: Pluto
HARDNESS: 7–7.5
WATER SAFE: No
ZODIAC: Scorpio
CHAKRA: Root
METAPHYSICAL PROPERTIES:
Protection, Grounding, EMF Shield

Turquoise

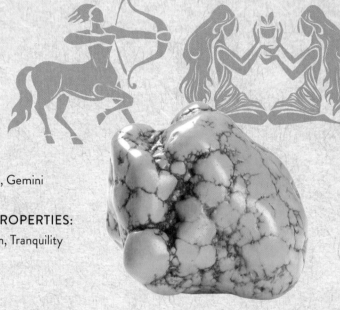

ELEMENT: Air
PLANET: Jupiter
HARDNESS: 5–7
WATER SAFE: No
ZODIAC: Sagittarius, Gemini
CHAKRA: Throat
METAPHYSICAL PROPERTIES:
Expression, Inspiration, Tranquility

Unakite

ELEMENT: Earth
PLANET: Venus
HARDNESS: 6–7
WATER SAFE: Yes
ZODIAC: Cancer, Pisces, Taurus
CHAKRA: Solar Plexus, Sacral
METAPHYSICAL PROPERTIES:
Balance, Grounding, Vision

CONCLUSION

Crystals can profoundly impact your spiritual practice and day-to-day life, but the real magic will always lie within *you*! Throughout this book, belief and intention are key elements and cannot be stressed enough. While crystals offer depth to our rituals and magic, remember to go at your own pace while learning what may or may not work for you.

The following pages include a crystal grid, moon, and spell worksheet. Make copies of these worksheets and use them as templates when you're creating your crystal grids and casting spells. I hope the information in this book guides and inspires you along your journey with the knowledge to select the crystals that best suit you and your purpose.

Blessed be!

Crystal Grid Worksheet

DATE: _____

DURATION: _____

MOON PHASE: _____

GEOMETRIC SHAPE: _____

GRID PURPOSE/INTENTION: _____

_____

_____

_____

_____

CRYSTALS: _____

_____

_____

_____

NOTES: _____

_____

_____

_____

_____

Moon Worksheet

MOON PHASE: _____

DATE: _____

TIME: _____

LOCATION: _____

INTENTION: _____
_____
_____
_____

SUPPLIES: _____
_____
_____
_____

RESULTS: _____
_____
_____

Spell Worksheet

SPELL NAME: _____

DATE: _____
TIME: _____
LOCATION: _____
MOON PHASE: _____

INTENTION: _____
_____
_____
_____

SUPPLIES: _____
_____
_____
_____

RESULTS: _____
_____
_____
_____

Recommended Reading

The Crystal Bible
Judy Hall

Crystal Muse
Heather Askinosie, Timmi Jandro

Crystals for Healing
Karen Frazier

The Crystal RX
Coleen McCann

Rise Sister Rise
Rebecca Campbell

The Encyclopedia of Crystals, Herbs, and New Age Elements
Adams Media

The Power of Crystals
Juliet Madison

The Witch
Lisa Lester

The Green Witch
Arin Murphy-Hiscock

Practical Magic: A Beginner's Guide to Crystals, Horoscopes, Psychics, and Spells
Nikki Van De Car, Tessa Netting

Online Resources

Earth Family Crystals
Blog
https://earthfamilycrystals.com/blogs

Daimonikos Productions
Services
www.daimonikosproductions.com

Anna Miranda
Training
www.annamiranda.net

Sacred Spaces
Services
www.sacredspacesli.com

The Sisters Enchanted
Podcast
www.thesistersenchanted.com

International Association of Reiki Professionals
Training
www.iarp.org

Acknowledgments

I am forever grateful for my best friend and partner in crime who supported me day and night throughout the writing of this book. His guidance, love and patience are unmatched. Thank you for keeping me safe and grounded. "You're my everything from here to Mars."

Thank you to my fellow witchy gals for their contributions and ongoing support throughout this project. I am honored to know such talented and intelligent women. And a very special thanks to Jackie Allen for her contributions.

Last but not least, thank you to Quarto Publishing for giving me the opportunity to share my thoughts, ideas, and what I love.

Author & Contributor Bios

Sara Hadley discovered her spiritual gifts and passion for healing ten years ago and began studying various healing, including Reiki. In 2017 she began her Reiki training and is now a Reiki Master Teacher. Sara's heart-centered approach comes from a place of deep empathy and care for her clients. Her intuitive gifts, passion for good vibes, and a balanced energy within the home have inspired her to share her knowledge with others. She strongly believes that we all have the power to create a fulfilling life for ourselves, and live with integrity in our hearts.

Courtney Pepino is the co-founder of Daimonikos Productions, a metaphysical, holistic healing, and cultural event business dedicated to promoting personal healing and spiritual discovery. She is a reiki practitioner, storyteller, educator, priestess, and co-founder of the Daimonikos Tradition. Courtney is happy to share her knowledge and expertise for *The Witch's Complete Guide to Crystals*.